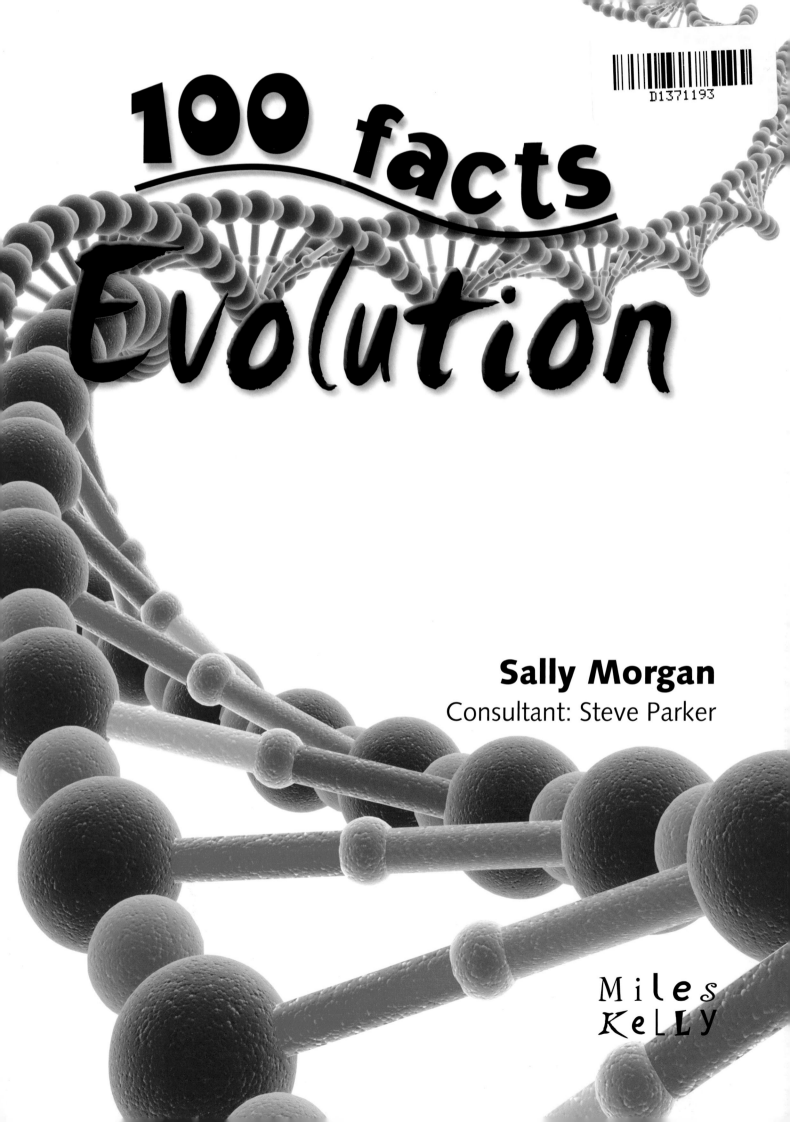

100 facts
Evolution

Sally Morgan

Consultant: Steve Parker

Miles Kelly

D1371193

First published in 2012 by Miles Kelly Publishing Ltd
Harding's Barn, Bardfield End Green, Thaxted, Essex, CM6 3PX, UK

Copyright © Miles Kelly Publishing Ltd 2014

This edition printed 2014

10 9 8 7 6 5 4 3

Publishing Director Belinda Gallagher
Creative Director Jo Cowan
Editorial Director Rosie Neave
Editor Claire Philip
Volume Designer Andrea Slane
Cover Designer Kayleigh Allen
Image Manager Liberty Newton
Indexer Gill Lee
Production Manager Elizabeth Collins
Reprographics Stephan Davis, Jennifer Cozens,
Thom Allaway
Assets Lorraine King

All rights reserved. No part of this publication may be reproduced,
stored in a retrieval system, or transmitted by any means, electronic,
mechanical, photocopying, recording or otherwise, without the prior
permission of the copyright holder.

ISBN 978-1-84810-563-8

Printed in China

British Library Cataloguing-in-Publication Data
A catalogue record for this book is available from the British Library

ACKNOWLEDGEMENTS

The publishers would like to thank the following artists
who have contributed to this book:
Julian Baker at JB Illustrations, Mike Foster at Maltings Partnership,
Stuart Jackson-Carter, Mike Saunders
All other artwork from the Miles Kelly Artwork Bank

The publishers would like to thank the following
sources for the use of their photographs:
t = top, b = bottom, l = left, r = right, c = centre, bg = background
Cover Front: Smetek/Science Photo Library, Back: Fotolia.com
Ardea 13(cr) Piers Cavendish, (b) Mary Clay; 34(bl) Jean Michel Labat
Corbis 18–19 Louie Psihoyos
Dreamstime.com 11(crab) Mailthepic
Fotolia.com 4(c); 5(bl) Kirsty Pargeter; 13(t) Darren Hester;
19, 22, 23, 32, 33, 34, 35 (paper) Alexey Khromushin
Getty Images 8(l) Jim Zuckerman; 38 Spencer Grant; 39(b) Ariadne
Van Zandbergen
iStockphoto.com 23(tr) Jouke van der Meer
FLPA 14(t) Rob Reijnen/Minden Pictures; 15(vegetarian free finch,
woodpecker finch) Tui De Roy/Minden Pictures; 17(br) Thomas
Marent/Minden Pictures; 36 Paul Sawer
Naturepl.com 9(b) Andy Rouse
Newscom 9(tl) Album/Prisma
NHPA 16 Gerard Lacz; 18(cl) Theodore Clutter
Rex Features 6–7(c); 7(b) Sipa Press; 19(tr) KeystoneUSA-ZUMA
Science Photo Library 4–5 Mark Garlick; 6–7(t); 12(br) Patrick Landmann;
20–21 Jose Antonio Peñas; 22–23, 26 Christian Jegou Publiphoto; 24 Alan
Sirulnikoff; 31(b) Jaime Chirinos; 32(t) Christian Darkin; 37(cl) Philippe
Psaila; 38(cl) Russell Kightly

Shutterstock.com 1 dream designs; 2 saiko3p; 3(t) donatas1205,
(b) David Thyberg; 6–7(bg) Mark Carrel; 6(tr), (br), 7(br) Andy Lidstone;
6–7 (c/bg) MalDix; 7(cr) donatas1205; 8(br) Brandelet; 9(t) Ragnarock;
10(clade bg) kanate, (t–b) Rostislav Ageev, Christopher Elwell, FAUP,
NatalieJean, Philip Lange, (bl) donatas1205; 11(bg) Mark Carrel,
(caption bg) sharpner, (tiger, lion, caracal, cat, cheetah, fox, sea lion,
gorilla, koala, frog) Eric Isselée, (weasel) Ronnie Howard, (wolf) Maxim
Kulko, (bat) Kirsanov, (whale) Computer Earth, (rabbit) Stefan Petru
Andronache, (polar bear) Ilya Akinshin, (hummingbird) Steffen Foerster
Photography, (sailfish) holbox, (crocodile) fivespots, (dragonfly) Subbotina
Anna, (frog) Arek Rainczuk, (snail) Sailorr, (eagle) Steve Collender,
(starfish) Mircea Bezergheanu, (jellyfish) Khoroshunova Olga,
(shark) Rich Carey, (snake) fivespots; 14(tiger) Uryadnikov Sergey,
(stags) Mark Bridger, (tadpoles) Paul Broadbent, (caption bg)
U.P.images_vector; 15(tr) donatas1205, (map) AridOcean,
(globe) Anton Balazh, (large ground finch, common cactus finch)
Stubblefield Photography; 17(globe) Anton Balazh; 18(bl) donatas1205;
21(panel) illustrart; 26–27(bg) Andre Mueller; 26(bl) donatas1205;
28–29 Pakhnyushcha; 29(bl) donatas1205; 30(bg) Lucy Baldwin;
(tr) FloridaStock; 33(cr) donatas1205, (caption bg) sharpner;
34–35(bg) Mark Carrel; 34–35(leather panels) saiko3p; 37 Dudarev
Mikhail; 39(t) Pasi Koskela
All other photographs are from:
Corel, digitalSTOCK, digitalvision, John Foxx, PhotoAlto, PhotoDisc,
PhotoEssentials, PhotoPro, Stockbyte

Every effort has been made to acknowledge the source
and copyright holder of each picture.
Miles Kelly Publishing apologises for any unintentional
errors or omissions.

Made with paper from a sustainable forest

www.mileskelly.net
info@mileskelly.net

CONTENTS

Life on Earth

1 Earth is about 4600 million years old. At first our planet could not support life. It was a mass of red-hot, liquid rock often battered by meteorites (rocks from space). Over millions of years Earth cooled down and conditions changed, making it possible for life to exist. The first organisms (life forms) appeared on Earth about 3500 million years ago.

▼ We don't know for certain what Earth looked like more than 3000 million years ago before life began. There were many volcanoes, but no oceans.

2 The first organisms were very simple – just a single cell. Cells are the tiny, basic building blocks of all living things. Over millions of years life has become incredibly varied and complex, adapting to Earth's ever-changing environments. For example, the animal kingdom includes birds, insects, fish, reptiles and mammals. This amazing development is called 'evolution'.

3 Evolution has been studied for more than one hundred years. In the 18th century, scientists such as Charles Darwin (1809–1882) started forming theories to explain the vast changes in life over time. Since then, scientists have continued to examine living things and fossils – the remains of once-living organisms preserved in rocks – to explain how evolution works.

Darwin's travels

4 Charles Darwin was one of the world's greatest scientists. His work on evolution changed people's ideas about life on Earth and it is still important today, influencing modern scientists.

▶ Charles Darwin joined HMS Beagle and sailed around the world when he was just 22 years old.

Despite its great weight, *Megatherium* could stand upright on two legs

5 The young Charles Darwin was a keen collector of beetles and fossils. He didn't do well in school and stopped studying medicine because he hated working on dead bodies. Darwin later went to Cambridge University to train to become a Christian priest, but some of his professors encouraged him to study living things instead.

▶ While at university, Darwin collected beetles, a popular craze of the time. These are some of the ones he gathered.

6 In 1831, Darwin joined HMS *Beagle* as the ship's naturalist. Naturalists are scientists that study animals and plants. Over the next five years, Darwin found many unknown species (types) of animals and plants. When HMS *Beagle* explored South America, Darwin saw volcanic eruptions, experienced earthquakes and discovered ancient animal remains.

▶ In Argentina, South America, Darwin found a complete fossil of an animal that he had never seen before. It was a giant ground sloth named *Megatherium*.

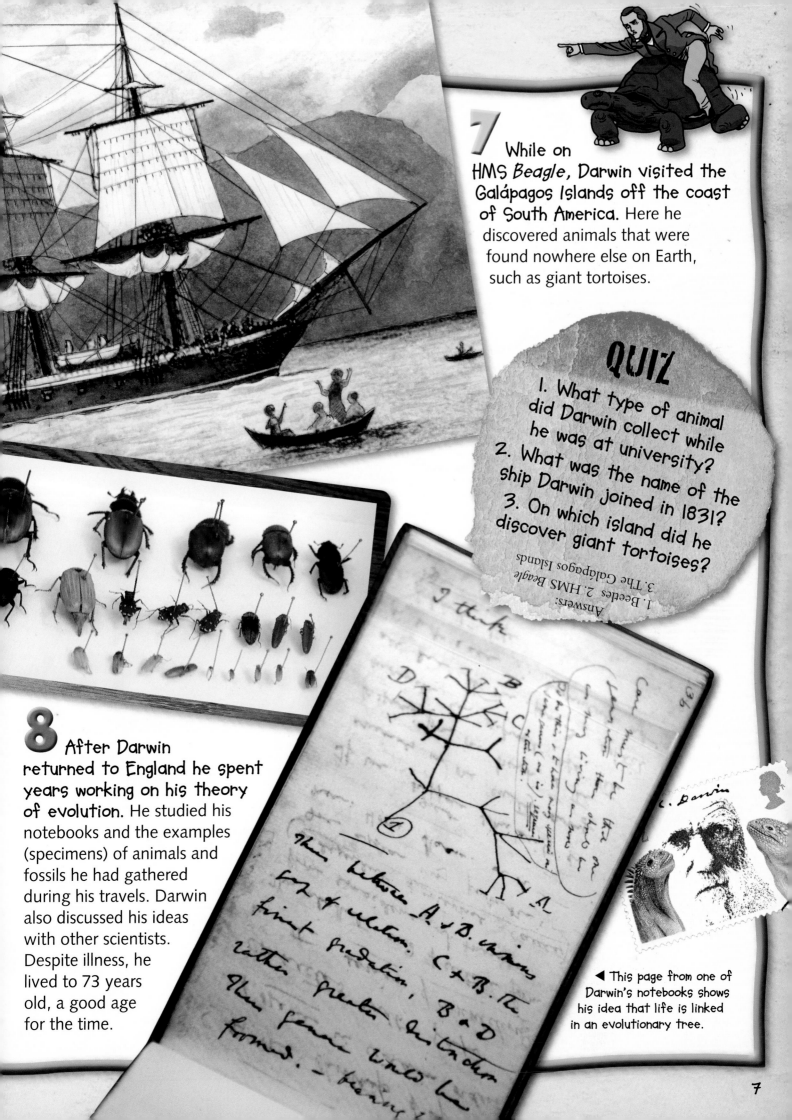

7 While on HMS *Beagle*, Darwin visited the Galápagos Islands off the coast of South America. Here he discovered animals that were found nowhere else on Earth, such as giant tortoises.

QUIZ

1. What type of animal did Darwin collect while he was at university?
2. What was the name of the ship Darwin joined in 1831?
3. On which island did he discover giant tortoises?

Answers:
1. Beetles 2. HMS *Beagle* 3.The Galápagos Islands

8 After Darwin returned to England he spent years working on his theory of evolution. He studied his notebooks and the examples (specimens) of animals and fossils he had gathered during his travels. Darwin also discussed his ideas with other scientists. Despite illness, he lived to 73 years old, a good age for the time.

◀ This page from one of Darwin's notebooks shows his idea that life is linked in an evolutionary tree.

The riddle of life

9 A species is a type of living thing. All the individuals of a species have a similar appearance. They can breed with each other to produce offspring (babies). There are millions of different species alive today, as well as millions that have become extinct (died out completely).

10 Darwin was not the first scientist to write about evolution. French scientist Jean-Bapiste Lamarck (1744–1829) had a theory that if an animal adapted to its environment during its lifetime, the changes would be passed on to its offspring. Although not entirely correct, his ideas sparked interest. Other scientists also began to question whether God had created species as they now exist.

◀ Lamarck falsely believed that if a giraffe stretched its neck to reach the highest leaves on a tree, its neck would get longer – and its offspring would have longer necks too.

▼ Each of these butterflies is a different species. They do not breed with each other and look different.

Brown argus

Purple emperor

Clouded yellow

Adonis blue

Green hairstreak

11 For centuries, people thought that a species could not change. Darwin examined mockingbirds from the Galápagos Islands and found differences between the specimens. He had an idea that the birds may have adapted to the islands' different environments. Darwin showed that a species could change over time and does not have a 'fixed' appearance.

▶ As Darwin explored the Galápagos Islands, he noticed small differences between the mockingbird species on each separate island.

12 In 1858, Alfred Russel Wallace (1823–1913), a fellow scientist, wrote to Darwin about his ideas on evolution. Darwin was horrified to discover that Wallace had similar theories to his own. This spurred Darwin into publishing his book, *On the Origin of Species* in 1859. Some people were very interested by its ideas, but others were outraged.

◀ This cartoon of Darwin with the body of an ape appeared in 1871 after he wrote that humans and apes had a common ancestor (relative from the past).

13 In 1871 Darwin published a second book entitled *The Descent of Man*. He wrote about the similarities and differences between humans and other apes, as well as the differences between humans from different cultures. Many people did not approve of the fact that Darwin had linked the evolution of people to that of chimpanzees.

▼ Darwin's theories about humans being related to other apes, such as chimps, are now accepted by most scientists.

14 Lots of people disagreed with Darwin, believing instead that God created all living things. This belief is called Creationism. Creationists believe that living organisms cannot produce new forms of life, and that only God can do this.

9

Classifying species

15 All living organisms are related and are linked in a huge web of life. To keep track of the vast number of species, living things can be classified (put into groups).

16 One method of classifying life is called cladistics. A clade is a group made up of an ancestor (a relative from the past) and all its living and extinct descendants, which developed from them. A clade is based on features that have been inherited, or passed on, from the ancestor. Usually, only the descendants have the specific feature.

COMMON ANCESTOR

Animals with stalks attached to the sea floor. Crinoids have cup-shaped bodies and many feathery arms

Crinoids

Large central disc and four or more radiating arms

Starfish

Star-shaped body with central disc and radiating arms

Smaller central disc than starfish and snake-like arms

Brittlestars

Moving animals with mouths on the underside of their bodies

▲ ECHINODERM CLADE
Echinoderms are a unique group of animals, which have a spiny skin and five or more arms that radiate (branch) out from a body made up of five equal parts.

Body covered in long spines

Sea urchins

Round body shape with no arms

Elongated body with leathery skin

Sea cucumbers

CLASSIFYING SHOES

You will need:
pen   notepad   lots of shoes
1. Divide the shoes into groups such as trainers, boots, wellies.
2. Separate each group into smaller groups, using features such as heels, laces and so on.
3. Keep dividing the groups until each shoe has its own group. Draw a chart to show how you classified the shoes.

17 All humans are related to the very first human beings. These first humans shared an ancestor with chimpanzees. If we look back further still, all primates – the animal group that includes monkeys and apes such as chimps and humans – share the same shrew-like, mammalian ancestor.

18 The scientist Carl Linnaeus (1707–1778) classified organisms in a clear, scientific way. He arranged species into groups according to their body features and gave each species a unique Latin name. Each name is made up of two words, for example, the tiger is *Panthera tigris*.

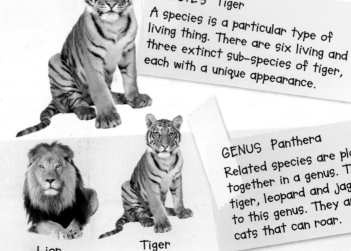

SPECIES Tiger
A species is a particular type of living thing. There are six living and three extinct sub-species of tiger, each with a unique appearance.

GENUS Panthera
Related species are placed together in a genus. The lion, tiger, leopard and jaguar belong to this genus. They are the only cats that can roar.

Lion   Tiger

FAMILY Felidae
The members of a family are closely related. There are 41 members of the felidae cat family.

Caracal   Domestic cat   Tiger   Cheetah

ORDER Carnivora
In an order, species are grouped together due to shared characteristics. Animals in the carnivora order are all meat-eating mammals.

Red fox   Tiger   Sea lion   Wolf
Weasel

CLASS Mammals
There are five vertebrate classes – birds, amphibians, reptiles, fish and mammals. All mammals have hair, breathe air and feed their young milk.

Bat   Whale   Gorilla   Tiger   Koala   Rabbit   Polar bear

PHYLUM Chordates
Animals are grouped in different phylums depending on their body structure. Chordates have a spinal cord. Most are vertebrates (backboned animals).

Frog   Sailfish
Hummingbird   Tiger   Crocodile

19 Scientists used to classify different species purely by their appearance. For example plants were grouped according to leaf shape, or the colour and number of their petals. The study of DNA (see page 12) made scientists change their ideas about evolution and reclassify many species.

Dragonfly   Toad   Snail   Eagle
Tiger
Starfish   Jellyfish   Shark   Snake   Crab

KINGDOM Animalia
All living things are placed into five main groups, including animals, plants and fungi.

DNA and genetics

I DON'T BELIEVE IT!

If all the DNA in your body was put end to end, it would reach from Earth to the Sun and back more than 660 times.

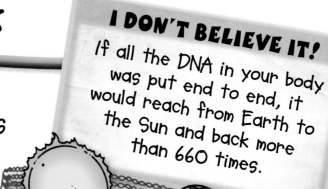

20 Inside most cells there is a substance called DNA. DNA stands for de-oxyribonucleic acid. It carries all the genes for a living thing. Genes are chemical instructions – they control all the processes in the body, such as growth and having offspring. DNA forms chromosomes, the tiny thread-like structures that are found in the nucleus (control centre) of a cell.

▼ Each chromosome is formed from one DNA molecule, and each DNA molecule contains many genes. A gene is a length of DNA with the code to do a particular job in a cell.

DNA strand

Gene

Each DNA molecule is formed from two strands joined together

Imagine DNA as a twisted ladder. The rungs are formed from chemicals called bases

Nucleus containing chromosomes

Chromosome

Cell

▼ In laboratories such as this, scientists examine DNA in a process called sequencing. They are able to find out the order of the four chemical bases that make up the individual genes.

21 The DNA of a chromosome is divided into genes. Each gene is a set of instructions in the form of a code – a bit like the code of a computer programme. These instructions tell the cell what to do.

22 Each new individual inherits its genes from its parents. The parental genes are shuffled so that the offspring has features from both parents. This creates variation, which is essential for evolution as it allows new features to develop. A clone is an individual that is genetically identical to another.

▲ All bananas from the same tree are clones of each other. They have the same DNA and so are genetically identical.

24 A gene exists in different forms. Usually there is a dominant and a recessive form. For example, one gene controls hair length in cats. Long hair is dominant and short hair is recessive. To be short-haired, a cat needs to inherit a recessive gene from both parents.

23 A mutation is a change within the DNA. If DNA is altered or damaged, its code is changed and a new form of the gene is created. Mutations are important as they can be inherited. If a species develops a useful characteristic, it will be passed on to its offspring.

▼ The female nine-banded armadillo usually has four offspring. They all come from one fertilized egg and so they are clones of each other.

▶ A recessive mutation produced this white tiger. White tigers cannot see as well as the normal orange tiger. As the mutation does not benefit the tiger, the gene is less likely to be passed on.

The struggle for survival

25 Many things can affect an animal's survival. For example, food supply, disease and climate. If there is a change, some individuals may survive the new conditions. The survivors pass on their favorable genes to their young – this is natural selection.

▲ Predators such as polar bears target their hunts at weak or sick animals. The healthier, fitter animals tend to survive and reproduce.

26 Natural selection can cause changes within a species. The ancestors of modern tigers may have had fewer stripes. Stripes give good camouflage as they help the animal blend in with its surroundings. The ancestors with the gene for more stripes may have been the most successful hunters, and so would have raised more offspring, passing on the genes for stripy coats.

▼▶ These are three of the different ways animals have evolved to ensure their genes are passed on.

APPEARANCE
A camouflaged appearance gives this tiger a natural advantage while hunting.

SEXUAL SELECTION
Stags with the biggest antlers and best fighting technique are more likely to win females and have young.

LOTS OF OFFSPRING
Some animals, such as toads, have to have lots of young as many won't survive to adulthood.

27 When species change due to natural selection, evolution takes place. This process of selection has led to all the different species alive today. It is also one reason species can become extinct, as the least successful animals die out.

QUIZ

1. Where are the Galápagos Islands?
2. Which shape of beak is good for feeding on nectar?
3. What does the word extinct mean?

Answers:
1. Off the coast of South America 2. Long and pointed 3. To have died out completely

28 If a species is separated and isolated this too can cause evolution. When a group of individuals is cut off from others of the same species, they can only breed with each other. As they adapt to the new local conditions they evolve into a new species, unable to breed with the original group they were separated from.

29 A group of animals can be isolated by a river, an ocean or a mountain range. The Galápagos Islands are isolated from South America by the Pacific Ocean. Thousands of years ago, a few finches were blown there by strong winds. They stayed on the islands and bred, evolving separately from the mainland birds.

▼▶ The Galápagos Islands provided a range of environments to which the finches adapted.

SOUTH AMERICA

Galápagos Islands

▼▶ There are about 14 different finch species on the Galápagos Islands. Each has a different beak shape suited to its particular diet.

Common cactus finch
Beak Long and pointed
Diet Nectar of cactus flowers

Large ground finch
Beak Large and thick
Diet Nuts, seeds and cactus fruits

Vegetarian tree finch
Beak Short, thick, parrot-like
Diet Plant buds, flowers, leaves

Woodpecker finch
Beak Pointed and narrow
Diet Insects and grubs

15

Looking for evidence

30 **To show how species evolve, scientists look for evidence.** They can examine and compare rocks, fossils and DNA for clues to back up their theories.

32 **The study of rocks can tell us about the climate on Earth millions of years ago.** Rocks that are rich in corals and the skeletons of other marine animals were formed when there were tropical oceans covering the land.

▼ Coelacanths (say 'seel-uh-kanths') were thought to be extinct until a living specimen was found in 1938. They are descended from the group of fish that evoved into amphibians.

Bony scales for protection not found on other live fish

Long, limb-like fins are used to 'walk' through the water

31 **Fossils tell us what plants and animals looked like millions of years ago.** Scientists compare living species with fossils of extinct species to see how much they have evolved over time.

33 **Scientists can extract DNA from living cells to read their genetic code.** The DNA of different organisms is compared to see how closely related they are. The most closely related have similar DNA.

◄ This fossil coelacanth shows that the fish has changed little over time.

Tenrecs are small, spiny animals found mostly in Madagascar. Their closest relatives are elephants and aardvarks

Prickly hedgehogs are found in Europe, Africa, parts of Asia and New Zealand

The echidna from Australia uses its long snout to find ants and termites

34 Some unrelated species have evolved similar traits. Animals in different parts of the world have evolved spines for protection, while hummingbirds, butterflies and possums all have long tongues for probing into flowers to reach nectar. This is called convergent evolution.

▲ Tenrecs, hedgehogs and echidnas are unrelated species, yet they have each evolved similar body features because they live in similar environments.

35 Where animals are found in the world tells us about how they evolved. When Madagascar became separated from Africa, lemurs (a type of primate) became isolated, and evolved separately from other African primates.

AFRICA

Madagascar

▲ Madagascar split from the coast of Africa about 165 million years ago.

▲ Lemurs, such as these ring-tailed lemurs, are only found in Madagascar.

Fossil clues

36 Fossils are the remains of living organisms that have been preserved in the ground. Most fossils are of animals, but plants can be fossilized too. The oldest fossils are of cyanobacteria (simple, single-celled organisms) that lived more than 3000 million years ago.

37 Fossil formation is a slow process. Some fossils can form in just 10,000 years, but most take much longer – usually hundreds of thousands, or even millions of years.

38 When an animal dies, its body might be buried under a layer of mud and sand. The soft body parts rot away but the hard parts, such as the bones, remain and become rock-like.

▼ The fossil magnolia (left) looks almost identical to the fruit from a living magnolia plant.

TRUE OR FALSE?

1. Fossils can be millions of years old.
2. The deeper the rock the younger the fossil.
3. Fossils helped Darwin work out his theory of evolution.

Answers:
1. True 2. False, usually the deeper the rock the older the fossil 3. True

▲ These palaeontologists (scientists who study the history of life on Earth) are working on an excavation or 'dig' in Wyoming in the United States, where dinosaur fossils have been found.

► These fossils were found in the La Brea Tar Pits near Los Angeles, United States. In the past, animals became trapped in the tar and died.

39 Scientists can learn how an extinct species lived by studying its fossil. For example, the structure and joints of an animal's legs shows how the animal walked, and how its muscles were attached to its skeleton.

40 The study of fossils helped Darwin work out his theory of evolution. He noticed that animal fossils found on islands such as the Cape Verde Islands and Falkland Islands in the Atlantic Ocean looked different from those he found on the South American mainland, giving him ideas about separation and isolation (see page 15).

41 Fossils can be dated to find out when they lived on Earth. One way is to work out of the age of the rock in which they were found. Usually, the deeper the rock, the older the fossil. To work out a fossil's absolute age, scientists make use of carbon-dating. All living things contain natural radioactivity, which leaks away at a steady rate. The amount remaining helps date the fossil.

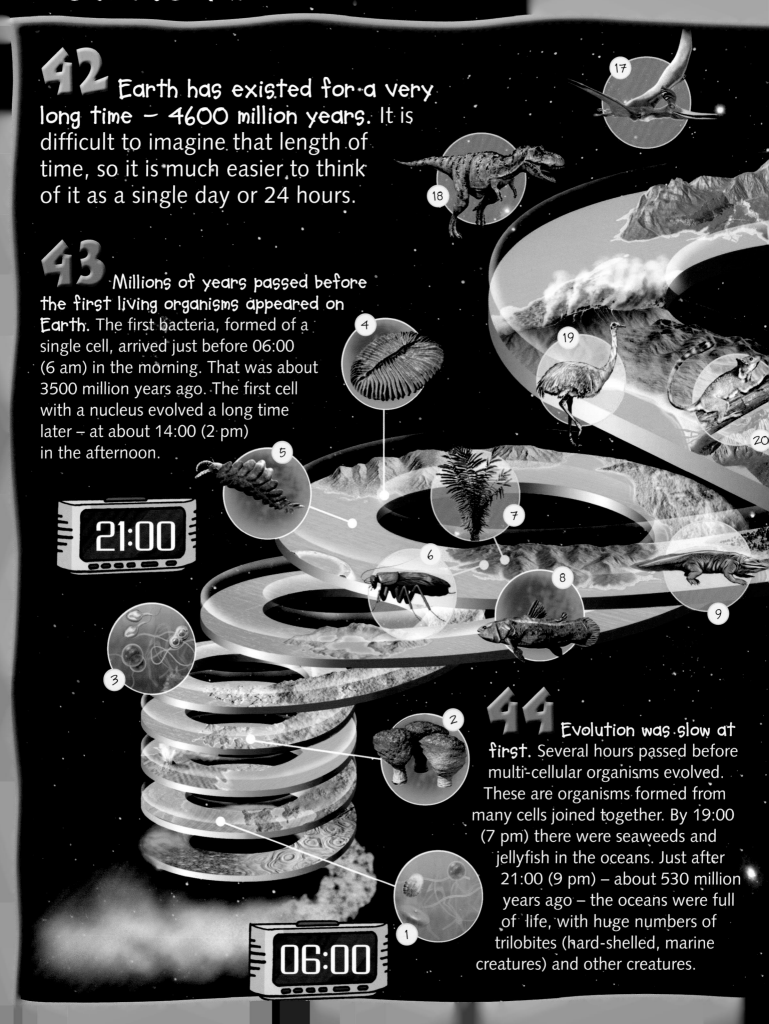

42 Earth has existed for a very long time — 4600 million years. It is difficult to imagine that length of time, so it is much easier to think of it as a single day or 24 hours.

43 Millions of years passed before the first living organisms appeared on Earth. The first bacteria, formed of a single cell, arrived just before 06:00 (6 am) in the morning. That was about 3500 million years ago. The first cell with a nucleus evolved a long time later – at about 14:00 (2 pm) in the afternoon.

44 Evolution was slow at first. Several hours passed before multi-cellular organisms evolved. These are organisms formed from many cells joined together. By 19:00 (7 pm) there were seaweeds and jellyfish in the oceans. Just after 21:00 (9 pm) – about 530 million years ago – the oceans were full of life, with huge numbers of trilobites (hard-shelled, marine creatures) and other creatures.

21:00

06:00

45 Animals moved onto land and by 22:00 (10 pm) there were insects flying in the sky. The dinosaurs ruled the Earth from about 23:00 (11 pm), while the first small, furry mammals appeared soon afterwards.

23:00

23:59

EVOLUTION THROUGH TIME KEY
1 Simple cells
2 Cyanobacteria
3 Cnidarians (soft-bodied animals)
4 Ediacaran (early marine animals)
5 Anomalocaris (arthropod – animals with segmented bodies and no backbone)
6 Cockroach (insect)
7 Cycad (cone-bearing plant)
8 Coelacanth (fish)
9 Diadectes (reptile-like amphibian)
10 Dimetrodon (small, early reptile)
11 Plesiosaur (marine reptile)
12 Lilienstennus (dinosaur)
13 Pteranodon (flying reptile)
14 Brachiosaur (large dinosaur)
15 Magnolia (flowering plant)
16 Archaeopteryx (early bird)
17 Quetzalcoatlus (pterosaur – flying reptile)
18 Tyrannosaurus rex (dinosaur)
19 Moa (flightless bird)
20 Plesiadapis (early mammal)
21 Indricotheres (rhinoceros-like mammal)
22 Sabre-tooth (carnivorous mammal)
23 Macrauchenia (hoofed mammal)
24 Wolf (carnivorous mammal)
25 Homo sapiens (modern man)

▲ This diagram shows the evolution of life from the very first organisms that appeared more than 3000 million years ago to modern humans.

46 It's difficult to believe that humans have been around for a relatively short time. Modern man arrived on Earth at just one minute to midnight, about 200,000 years ago.

47 Understanding the evolutionary clock helps scientists work out the speed at which evolution takes place. Over the last 4600 million years, species have appeared and then disappeared, to be replaced by other species more suited to the changing environments.

The start of life

Frequent
volcanic
activity

48 For a few hundred million years, Earth was a hot mass of molten rock and gases. The atmosphere – the layer of gases that surrounds the Earth – contained water vapour, carbon dioxide and nitrogen but no oxygen. Gradually, the surface cooled, clouds formed and water vapour fell as rain. Rain poured onto the land to create the oceans.

◄ The Earth looked very different 3000 million years ago, during a period known as the Archaean. Much of the planet was covered by oceans.

49 Once there were oceans, conditions became more suited to the evolution of living things. The first building blocks of life appeared – amino acids, proteins and DNA. There are many theories about how these chemicals were created and how they joined up to form cells, but nobody knows for sure. It is one of the greatest mysteries.

Deep sea
vents

Stromatolites

50 The cooling continued and by about 3500 million years ago the first cells had evolved. These first cells were cyanobacteria. They grew in the sunny parts of the ocean and used sunlight to make food. During this process, cyanobacteria released oxygen into the atmosphere.

▼ Stromatolites, a type of cyanobacteria, are among the earliest fossils. They can still be seen at Shark Bay, Australia.

51 For the next 2500 to 3000 million years, life was very simple. There was bacteria, simple animals and plants, but no animals with a head, body and tail.

Jellyfish

▶ The first animals were soft bodied like jellyfish. *Charnia* was a strange animal that looked more like a plant.

Charnia

I DON'T BELIEVE IT!
Some scientists believe that Earth has twice been completely covered with ice. The last time they think this happened was 635 million years ago.

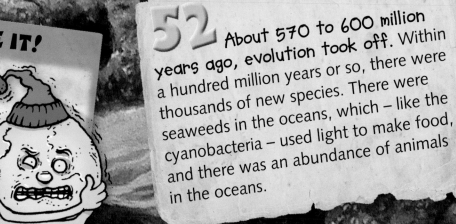

52 About 570 to 600 million years ago, evolution took off. Within a hundred million years or so, there were thousands of new species. There were seaweeds in the oceans, which – like the cyanobacteria – used light to make food, and there was an abundance of animals in the oceans.

Early animals

53 Fossils show that there were some very unusual animals living in the oceans about 500 million years ago. Some had several heads, trunks like elephants, backward-facing mouths, and many other odd features.

Opabinia

▼ Animals from the Cambrian Period died out when conditions on Earth changed. There are no living relatives.

Pikaia

54 Thousands of fossils have been found at the Burgess Shale deposits in Canada. The site was discovered in 1909 by Charles Walcott (1850–1927). He dug up more than 65,000 fossils. Amazingly, some were of soft-bodied animals such as jellyfish.

▼ These scientists are working on a dig in the famous Walcott Quarry in the Burgess Shale deposits, Canada.

Ottoia

Pirania

55 The oceans were full of life during the Cambrian Period (545–495 million years ago). There were molluscs, echinoderms, trilobites, worms, jellyfish and some early fish. Fish were different from the other animals as they had backbones – they were the first vertebrate animals.

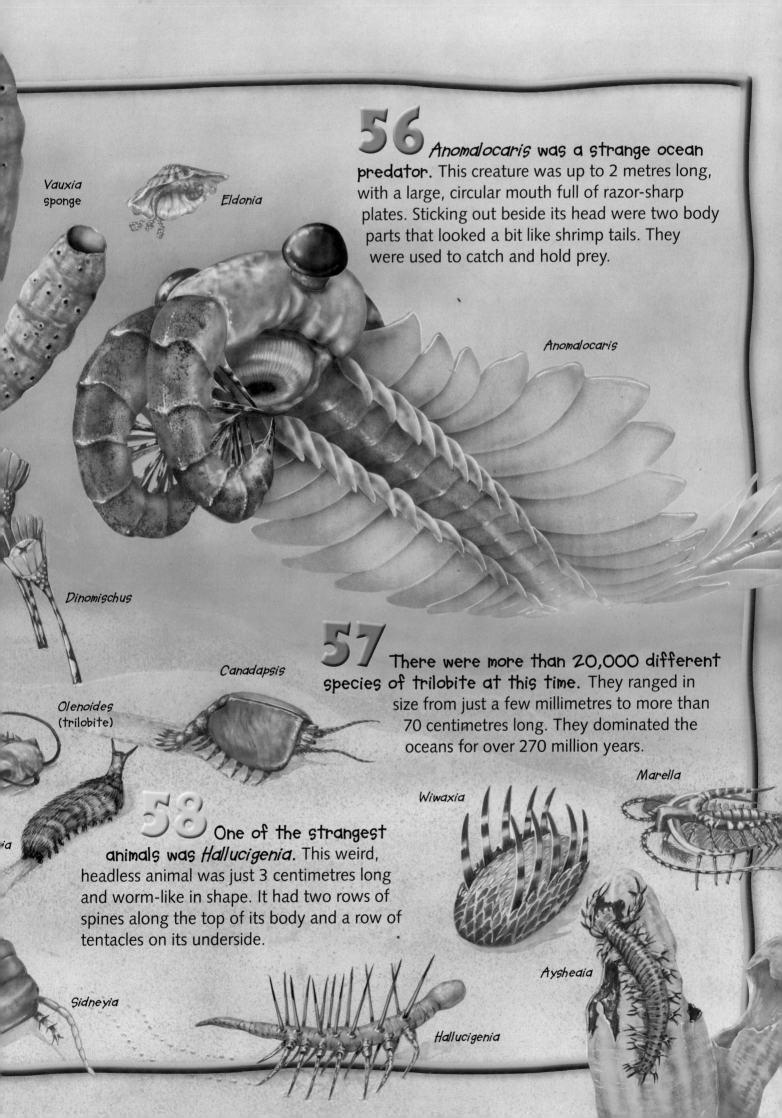

56 *Anomalocaris* was a strange ocean predator. This creature was up to 2 metres long, with a large, circular mouth full of razor-sharp plates. Sticking out beside its head were two body parts that looked a bit like shrimp tails. They were used to catch and hold prey.

Vauxia sponge

Eldonia

Anomalocaris

Dinomischus

Canadapsis

57 There were more than 20,000 different species of trilobite at this time. They ranged in size from just a few millimetres to more than 70 centimetres long. They dominated the oceans for over 270 million years.

Olenoides (trilobite)

Marella

Wiwaxia

58 One of the strangest animals was *Hallucigenia*. This weird, headless animal was just 3 centimetres long and worm-like in shape. It had two rows of spines along the top of its body and a row of tentacles on its underside.

Aysheaia

Sidneyia

Hallucigenia

Moving onto land

59 Simple plants first appeared about 400 million years ago. Mosses are primitive plants that can only grow in damp areas. Ferns are more highly evolved – they appeared 350 million years ago. By around 300 million years ago much of the land was covered conifer forests and swamps.

▲ This scene shows some early tree and plant species in a flooded forest during the Carboniferous Period (359–299 million years ago).

60 Most of the first land animals were plant eaters. One was *Arthropleura*, the largest ever millipede-like animal. Although it was related to arthropods such as insects and crabs, it grew to the size of a crocodile, with a body up to 2 metres in length.

61 Imagine a scorpion larger than you! This was *Pterygotus*, a fearsome predator that hunted fish more than 400 million years ago. Some of its relatives were among the first animals to crawl onto land. Sea scorpions are extinct, but they were the ancestors of the arachnid animal group that includes spiders and scorpions.

▼ Fossil footprints of *Arthropleura* have been found in rocks, showing the animals moved quickly over the ground.

EVOLVING ANIMALS

You will need:
pencil   notepad   tracing paper

1. Draw a simple outine of an animal.
2. Make a copy using tracing paper, but change one body part.
3. Trace the second picture. This time change something else.
4. Do this ten times, then look at your drawings to see how the animal evolved.

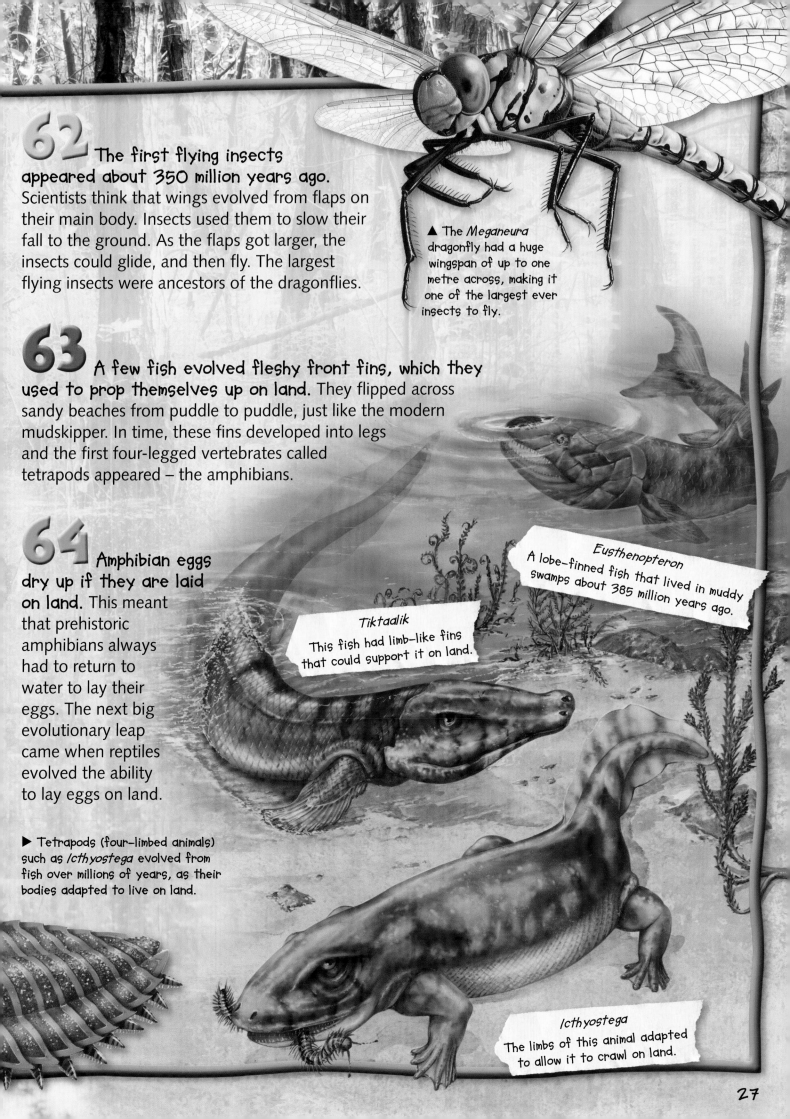

62 The first flying insects appeared about 350 million years ago. Scientists think that wings evolved from flaps on their main body. Insects used them to slow their fall to the ground. As the flaps got larger, the insects could glide, and then fly. The largest flying insects were ancestors of the dragonflies.

▲ The *Meganeura* dragonfly had a huge wingspan of up to one metre across, making it one of the largest ever insects to fly.

63 A few fish evolved fleshy front fins, which they used to prop themselves up on land. They flipped across sandy beaches from puddle to puddle, just like the modern mudskipper. In time, these fins developed into legs and the first four-legged vertebrates called tetrapods appeared – the amphibians.

64 Amphibian eggs dry up if they are laid on land. This meant that prehistoric amphibians always had to return to water to lay their eggs. The next big evolutionary leap came when reptiles evolved the ability to lay eggs on land.

▶ Tetrapods (four-limbed animals) such as *Icthyostega* evolved from fish over millions of years, as their bodies adapted to live on land.

Eusthenopteron
A lobe-finned fish that lived in muddy swamps about 385 million years ago.

Tiktaalik
This fish had limb-like fins that could support it on land.

Icthyostega
The limbs of this animal adapted to allow it to crawl on land.

Reptiles and dinosaurs

65 The very first reptiles developed from amphibians around 315 million years ago. They were small, lizard-like animals that laid eggs with a leathery shell. This adaption meant that they could live in dry habitats. They moved onto land where few animals had ventured before.

▲ One of the first reptiles was *Hylonomus*, a small, lizard-like animal. It laid eggs on land.

▲ Over millions of years, more than 1000 different dinosaur species evolved as they adapted to Earth's changing environments.

66 Dinosaurs evolved about 230 million years ago from a group of crawling reptiles. Dinosaurs ruled the Earth for about 170 million years, outnumbering the many other backboned creatures that lived at the same time.

67 The first dinosaurs, such as *Eoraptor*, were small, upright and ran on their back legs. Their upright posture was possible because they developed different hips from other reptiles. They could place their legs directly under their body to raise it off the ground. This allowed them to move faster.

68 The smallest dinosaurs weighed just a few kilograms, but there were some giants too. One of the largest was *Argentinosaurus*, which scientists think was about 40 metres long and weighed up to 50 tonnes. It is difficult to be sure as complete skeletons are rarely found.

▼ For about 100 million years enormous dinosaurs called sauropods, including *Argentinosaurus*, roamed the planet.

▶ *Giganotosaurus* was one of the largest carnivorous dinosaurs. Like *Argentinosaurus*, it lived in South America.

69 One of the most well known dinosaurs is *T rex*. It was one of the largest land carnivores that ever existed. *T rex* stood up on its hind legs and used its long tail to balance. It was 4 metres high at the hips and about 13 metres long. Despite its size, it was not quite as large as its relative *Giganotosaurus*.

▲ Near the end of the dinosaur's reign, sauropods were replaced by the plant-eating *Triceratops* (I), *Ankylosaurus* (2) and the duck-billed dinosaurs (3).

QUIZ

I. When did the first reptiles appear?
2. Was *Triceratops* a plant or meat eater?
3. For how long did dinosaurs rule the land?

Answers:
1. 315 million years ago 2. A plant eater 3. About 170 million years

70 About 65 million years ago a huge number of living things died out in a short time. This was probably caused by a meteor smashing into Earth, throwing up vast amounts of dust into the atmosphere and causing a global winter. More than half of the world's species could not survive the sudden changes and became extinct, including nearly all large land animals.

The first birds

Bald eagle

71 About 150 million years ago a small type of dinosaur evolved feathers and the ability to fly. Many scientists believe this dinosaur became the first bird. Birds are more closely related to the dinosaurs than dinosaurs are to modern-day crocodiles because they share a common ancestor.

Velociraptor

Talons for grabbing prey

▲ *Velociraptor* had hands and feet with curved claws, similar to the talons of modern-day birds of prey.

Long tail

▶ Scientists are not sure whether *Archaeopteryx* could flap its wings or just glide from tree to tree.

72 Darwin suspected that birds and dinosaurs were linked. In 1861, just two years after *On the Origin of Species* was published, the fossil skeleton of a bird-like creature, *Archaeopteryx*, was discovered. It had features of both dinosaurs, such as teeth and a bony tail, and birds, such as wings.

73 Birds share many features with reptiles. Reptiles have scaly skin, and scales can still be seen on the legs of birds. Both birds and reptiles lay eggs with a shell. Birds are thought to be descended from small, raptor-like dinosaurs called 'maniraptorans', which includes the *Velociraptor*.

Long flight feathers

Wing claws

Lightweight body

Toothed beak

◀ The feathers, claws and skull of *Archaeopteryx* can be seen clearly on fossils of this prehistoric creature.

74 There are many theories to explain why dinosaurs grew feathers. Birds use feathers for flying and for signalling to each other. As dinosaurs did not have wings, the first feathers may have had a different role – to provide warmth. After the dinosaurs evolved feathers, they became coloured for communication. They were used later for flight.

Feathers

▲ Dinosaurs such as *Guanlong* may have had brightly coloured feathers to attract mates.

75 After the age of the dinosaurs, the terror birds became the biggest predators. The earliest terror birds were chicken-sized, but a much larger bird called *Phorusrhacos* evolved on the grasslands of South America. This large, ostrich-like bird was more than 3 metres tall and could run at speeds of more than 60 kilometres an hour. The last survivors died out about 5000 years ago.

I DON'T BELIEVE IT!
The prehistoric-looking cassowary from Australia has stiff feathers and small wings. Its ancestors could fly, but over millions of years cassowaries have lost the ability to take to the sky.

▶ *Gastornis* was a fearsome predator with its crushing beak and clawed feet.

76 One of the largest birds that ever lived was the huge, flightless *Gastornis*. This giant, meat-eating bird stood more than 2 metres tall. It was equipped with an amazing weapon – a large, hatchet-shaped beak. It could crush the backbone of a small horse with just one bite.

Mammals take over

77 The first mammals evolved about 220 million years ago, and existed alongside the dinosaurs. They evolved from a different group of reptiles to dinosaurs and birds, called therapsids. The first mammals were small and weasel-like, and they probably hunted insects.

▶ The small, early mammal *Leptictidium* used its long snout to sniff out prey such as this cicada.

78 The rise of mammals was not quick – it took millions of years for them to develop and become more varied. Just like the dinosaurs before them, mammals evolved to suit many different habitats. Some returned to the sea in the form of whales and dolphins, others evolved long legs and roamed the grasslands, while bats developed wings and took to the air.

79 All mammals have the same arrangement of bones in their limbs. This is called the pentadactyl limb. The basic plan in the arm is a single bone in the upper limb (the humerus), which is jointed to two bones in the lower limb (the radius and the ulna). Each limb ends in five digits.

▼ The pentadactyl limb in each of these mammals has evolved so that it is adapted to suit their lifestyle.

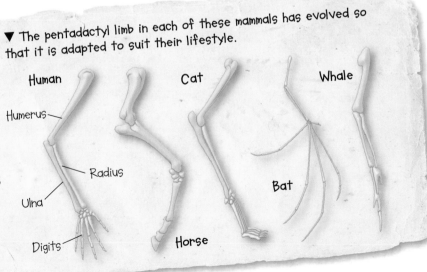

Human

Cat

Whale

Humerus

Radius

Ulna

Bat

Digits

Horse

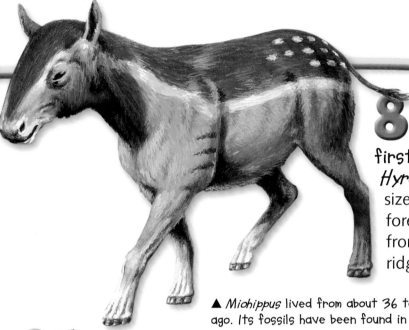

80 Around 50 million years ago the first horse-like animal appeared – *Hyracotherium*. These forest animals were the size of dogs. When grasslands replaced the forests, animals such as *Miohippus* took over from the *Hyracotherium*. *Miohippus* had large, ridged teeth for chewing tough grasses.

▲ *Miohippus* lived from about 36 to 25 million years ago. Its fossils have been found in North America.

81 Some amazing mammals lived during the last Ice Age, about 70,000 years ago. They adapted to survive in the extreme cold, as much of the land was covered in ice. Woolly mammoths lived alongside the sabre-tooth. This big cat was more like a bear in size and hunted bison and small mammoths.

QUIZ

Which of the following mammals is the odd one out?

Tiger Seal Horse Echidna
Bat Whale Dog Horse

Answer:
Echidna, the rest are placental mammals

82 There are almost 5500 species of mammal alive today. The most primitive are the egg-laying monotremes, such as the echidna, which share many characteristics with their reptilian ancestors. Marsupials such as the kangaroo and koala give birth to tiny babies that they care for in their pouch. The biggest group is the placental mammals, which give birth to well-developed young.

▶ Seals are placental mammals. The females are pregnant for one year and feed their young on milk.

▶ Marsupial mammals such as kangaroos carry their young around in a pouch.

There are only two monotreme mammals, the echidna (right) and the duck-billed platypus.

The human story

83 Humans belong to the primate mammal group. All primates have a large brain for their size, with forward-facing eyes that give 3D vision. Most primates have fingers with nails that are used for manipulating and grasping objects.

Forward-facing eyes

Large brain

► Primates include lemurs, monkeys and apes such as gibbons, chimps and gorillas (shown here).

Fingers with nails

Ardipithecus ramidus
4.4 million years ago

84 The first primates appeared about 75 million years ago. Humans have a common ancestor with chimps that lived in Africa about six million years ago. Then the line splits, with chimps evolving separately to humans. Four million years ago, our human ancestors were still tree dwellers that tottered on two legs.

Australopithecus afarensis
3.9–2.9 million years ago

► This timeline shows how various human groups have evolved, from very early kinds that lived in Africa over four million years ago, to modern humans.

Australopithecus africanus
2–3 million years ago

▼ A human's pelvis is shorter and wider than a gorilla's. It allows humans to stand upright.

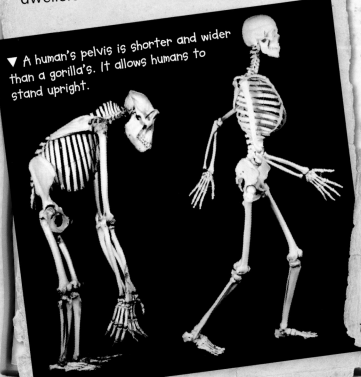

85 Two-and-a-half million years ago, the first human ancestor to use tools appeared. *Homo habilis* had a large brain and was very adaptable. It ate a varied diet, scavenging meat rather than eating grasses and learnt to use stone tools to smash bones to get at the rich marrow inside.

86 Two million years ago, one group of early humans moved out of Africa, and populated other regions of the world. This ancestor was *Homo erectus*, and it had a more human-like appearance. It lived in a variety of different habitats and learnt how to use fire and cook food.

I DON'T BELIEVE IT!

In 1974, scientists found fossilized bones in Ethiopia, Africa. The bones were 3.2 million years old and belonged to a small female creature. Scientists called her Lucy but her Latin name is *Australopithecus afarensis*.

87 Neanderthal people lived in Europe about 130,000 years ago. Europe was still in an Ice Age at this time. The Neanderthals had a short, stocky body, which was adapted for living in the cold. They hunted animals and ate a mostly meat diet. Then about 30,000 years ago, the climate got warmer, humans from Africa arrived and the Neanderthals died out.

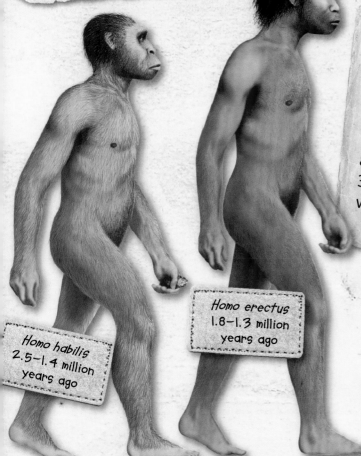

Homo habilis
2.5–1.4 million years ago

Homo erectus
1.8–1.3 million years ago

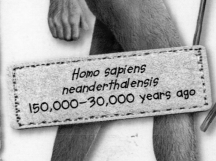

Homo sapiens neanderthalensis
150,000–30,000 years ago

Homo sapiens sapiens
200,000 to present

88 The modern human, with a highly developed brain, originated in Africa about 200,000 years ago. Like many other early humans, modern humans proved to be highly adaptable. They developed a culture and language, and learnt to depend on tools to alter their environment.

Designer evolution

89 People can alter evolution through artificial selection. This is similar to natural selection, but it involves people selecting the parents of the next generation. Over time, artificial selection can lead to new types of plants and animals.

90 The pet dog is related to the wolf. About 15,000 years ago, people started to tame the wolves that were found around their settlements. Over time, the appearences of the tamed animals changed as people selected parent dogs with particular features.

▼ Dogs can be grouped according to their appearance and the purpose for which they were bred.

GUNDOG
Irish setter

HOUND
Irish wolfhound

TERRIER
Jack Russell

TOY
Chihuahua

UTILITY
Bulldog

WORKING
Old English sheepdog

▲ Wolves are ancestors of all dog breeds. Wolves and dogs still have many features in common such as howling and barking.

91 The many different dog breeds look very different, but they are all the same species. This means they can breed with each other. There are different breeds of pet cats too, each bred for a particular appearance.

92 Artificial selection has developed crops and livestock too. By choosing parent plants with high yields or disease resistance, scientists have changed crop plants, such as wheat and rice. Dairy cows are now producing more milk, as farmers breed from cows that produce the most milk.

I DON'T BELIEVE IT!

More than 47,000 aspen trees in Utah, United States are joined by underground suckers. The parent tree sent out suckers from its roots, which sprouted into new trees. They are identical clones.

93 The most beneficial characteristics are chosen during artificial selection. Because most living things have two parents, they show variation (see page 13). This gives some individuals an advantage. For example, some plants have genes that make them grow taller, allowing them to reach sunlight more easily than other plants.

94 Clones can also be made by artificial selection. They are at an evolutionary disadvantage, however, because there is no variation between the individuals. If a group of cloned animals or plants are affected by disease, they could all be wiped out.

▲ Plant breeding can produce crop plants with more flavour, greater yields and more resistance to disease.

▼ Modern varieties of rice have greater yields. The latest types have been genetically altered so they survive in drought and salt water conditions.

Evolution in action

95 Evolution never stops – it is taking place around us right now. Usually, it occurs slowly, over millions of years. It took modern humans six million years to evolve from forest-dwelling animals. But sometimes evolution can happen in just a few years – or even less.

96 By understanding evolution, scientists have a better chance of fighting diseases. Humans can be vaccinated against influenza ('flu), a disease caused by a virus. The virus can evolve quickly, meaning scientists must keep developing new vaccines to keep up.

◀ Influenza vaccines no longer work when mutations change the surface of the influenza virus.

97 Farmers use weedkillers on their crops, but some weeds are becoming resistant. When a crop is sprayed, any weed that has a gene for resistance to the weedkiller survives, while the others die. This survivor produces seeds and soon there are more resistant weeds.

▶ The excessive use of weedkillers can cause some weeds to evolve a resistance to the chemicals.

▲ Mosquitoes carry parasites that cause malaria. The rise in global temperatures means they can now survive in more places.

98 The world's climate is changing and this is affecting evolution. Species with more variation can adapt to the changes and survive, while those that can't keep up are in danger of dying out. Climate change is also affecting the arrival of the seasons – in many places, spring is starting earlier. This is causing problems for plants and animals that depend on each other for survival.

99 Some lizards are changing their appearance to escape ants. Fire ants are small but aggressive and can kill the small fence lizard. Lizards that live close to these ants have longer legs than those that live in areas without the ants. Genes for long legs have been inherited to help the lizards escape.

▲ Long-legged fence lizards are more likely to survive and breed than the short-legged ones.

▼ The Hadza tribe of Africa are one of the few remaining hunter-gather tribes living in a way similar to our ancient ancestors.

100 Humans have evolved over the last few thousand years. Many adults cannot drink milk due to the lactose (sugar) it contains. About 5000 years ago, Europeans began keeping cattle. A mutation occured that allowed adults to digest the lactose. Human beings are an adaptable species – our ability to change may help us to survive in an ever-changing world.

Index